Saving America
Statesman Party Agenda

Daniel Wayne Orr

DEDICATION

To my daughters, Freya Brighton, Haley Rae, Faith Alexis & Lara Danielle, may you know that for you, I have endeavored to leave this world a better place than how I found it. May you do the same for yours.

CONTENTS

Daniel Wayne Orr

Appendix & Forms

ACKNOWLEDGMENTS

The words you find here are my own musings. But I am the product of every person who has ever stopped to talk about social policies, societal problems, government or the lack thereof. To that end, I wish to acknowledge, some of, the people who I revere as my influences. They made me think, research and develop my beliefs that I share here with you. I will limit these influences to those of good ideals. Family members Elizabeth Orr, Michael Orr, Estelle Hobgood, and Haley Orr. Presidents James Madison, John Adams, Abraham Lincoln, Thomas Jefferson, John Kennedy, Ronald Reagan, and my favorite Theodore Roosevelt. Philosophers Epictetus, Aristotle, Sophocles, and Siddhārtha Gautama. Educators Rupert Nacoste, Oliver Adunka, Virginia Aldige and Anita Flick. Finally, Oliver Wendell Holmes Sr., Robert Heinlein, and oddly enough, Douglas Adams. My friends Franca Russo Rivera, Lloyd Lenormand, John Capps, Chris Hines, David Gill, and most of all Nicholas Hendley. I am confident none of these people would agree in entirety with anything I convey here but I hope that I might get a nod or two that I learned something from each of them.

"Everything begins with just one person who believes, shares and works to an end."

Daniel Orr

From the internet: "An activist is someone who cannot help but fight for something. That person is not usually motivated by a need for power, money or fame but in fact is driven slightly mad by some injustice, some cruelty, some unfairness, so much so that he or she is compelled by some internal moral engine to act to make it better."

"Judicial abuse occurs when judges substitute their own political views for the law." - **Lamar S. Smith**

1 JUDICIAL BRANCH

One third of our government exists to ensure we are all equal and held accountable to law. While media and politicians point to the legislative and executive branches it is the judicial branch that continues to fail our American society. I see this as the greatest threat to our country.

Therefore this is the most longwinded of my political manifesto. If you wish to see the solutions without the rhetoric please skip down to page twenty-two (22).

Our second President of the United States of America was John Adams. Adams reluctantly came to see that the traditional colonial approach of Ministerial Government by England did not serve the settlers and pioneers that braved a new continent.

The original concept was the pursuit of personal property on which to flourish. Everything in Europe was claimed but here was a vast continent which despite its indigenous inhabitants was considered open and free. That desire for land evolved into the idea of a fresh start and was penned as "The pursuit of happiness."

John Adams wrote anonymously for years in support of the growing revolutionaries. Eventually he would come out of the shadows and place his reputation at risk to support the idealistic yet growing necessity of a new government that served and protected the people of this new land. Adams was regarded as a brilliant and blunt-spoken man. Placing his successful career in jeopardy and hiding his family from retaliation, Adams delivered his ideals and served the likeminded people that wanted something better. The risks he endured was recognized to be a considerable personal sacrifice earning him a place as a Founding Father and Patriot. England would regard him as criminal, traitor, and terrorist.

John Adams reputations grew in the media of the time. Essays he published during the 1770s and 1780s had colonists regarding him as an independent mind separate from the propaganda of English loyalists.

Some of today's Americans believe the ideas for our government were born here on our soil. Most Americans haven't truly given any thought or consideration to the idea at all. They merely complain at the squeeze they feel when their 'happiness', which is newly defined as comfort and not land, is obstructed.

Adam wrote "Thoughts on Government" (1776) which argued that the various functions of government had to be separated in order to avoid and prevent tyranny. The idea of a three part government – executive, judiciary, and legislative was gleaned from the English scholar John Locke born August 29th, 1692. Locke wrote extensively about Natural Rights and against the established "Divine Rights of Kings." The Divine Rights of Kings was the idea that God gave a bloodline the authority over a people. To disagree with this Head of the Bloodline was to go against the will of God. This was a powerful tool in enforcing the traditional government.

The new divine right of kings are the hidden powers of wealth that throw up smoke screens calling it in societies best interest to deprive individuals liberty. Later we will discuss how criminals and lawyers are the pawns and armies of these wealthy people.

Our Founding Fathers, including John Adams, were very influenced by Locke's writings. The guiding concept was that the People had natural rights. Considering this foremost lead to the radical ideal that to be governed, a government must obtain permission of the people governed. This was how the United States Constitution was structured. Natural Rights began with ownership of self. To allow someone else to make decisions was to lend not give away that ownership of self. That authority came from individuals who in theory had rights to defend and hold accountable those people to which they had given authority to.

Those people in authority also had the right and responsibility to hold one another in check. Here in lies the shrouded truth to the present day woes of our United States of America. Our government no longer checks each other but instead turned that authority over to the Judicial Branch to decide. Making that third more powerful than intended. History is confirming Lord Acton, "power corrupts and absolute power corrupts absolutely."

The intent was that attorneys would explain the law and a wise citizen judge would make a decision. But in the 1980s lawyers had made it to where only other lawyers could be judges compromising our legal system to cronyism and a faction of elite citizenry.

Wisdom was removed from this critical part of government and replaced with an educational requirement to limit participation and create a faction of elite citizens with wealth and political connections in what was supposed to be a non-partisan branch of government. The will of the people has been compromised. Modern day judges do not even pretend to follow the law. They use a collection of other corrupted court cases and call it 'common law' and insist that it trumps legislative law, "the people's law."

Ronald Dworkin, a scholar of constitutional law, is the second most cited legal scholar of the twentieth century. One of Dworkin's ideas exemplifies against the use of common law. He argues that the moral principles that judges self-assert are often wrong, so much so that a judges' abuse of discretion can be seen that certain crimes are acceptable if the judge's principles are skewed enough.

Dworkin postulates that judge's decisions are predetermined then qualified; bolstered by previous interruptions of legisled law or by abuses of discretion that previously slipped through. To discover and apply these principles, judges cherry pick and call it interpreting the legal data (legislation, cases etc.) with a view to articulating an interpretation that best explains and justifies their desire from past legal practice without regard to the actual legislated law of the people. With over two hundred years of mixed court decisions a judge essentially has the ability to pick anything he wants, not by wisdom but by faction loyalty. His decisions will stick because of the cronyism and faction loyalty that is entrenched in the judicial branch.

One very recent example in North

Carolina's 10th Superior Court district was that Wake County Superior Court Judge Paul Gessner ruled on 10/28/2013 that in a suit for "Willful Failure to Discharge Duties" directed at the Police Chief Cassandra Deck-Brown for refusing to have the Raleigh Police investigate the sexual abuse of a mentally ill woman by a known felon.

Gessner dismissed the suit, which called for a trial by jury, in the show cause portion of due process and created a gatekeeper order to prevent the plaintiff from filing cases against the police chief. Gessner asserted a plaintiff had to sue the city and not the public official. While North Carolina General Statutes § 14-230 states the law as "If any clerk of any court of record, sheriff, magistrate, school board member, county commissioner, county surveyor,

coroner, treasurer, or official of any of
the State institutions, or of any county,
city or town, shall willfully omit, neglect
or refuse to discharge any of the duties
of his office, for default whereof it is
not elsewhere provided that he shall be
indicted, he shall be guilty of a Class 1
misdemeanor. If it shall be proved that
such officer, after his qualification,
willfully and corruptly omitted,
neglected or refused to discharge any of
the duties of his office, or willfully and
corruptly violated his oath of office
according to the true intent and
meaning thereof, such officer shall be
guilty of misbehavior in office, and shall
be punished by removal therefrom
under the sentence of the court as a part
of the punishment for the offense."

Nowhere in the law does it say sue
the city it says hold the offender

accountable. This was nothing less than Judge Gessner, the judicial branch, protecting illegal / criminal activity by other members of the Judicial Branch. Supporting their faction and elite citizenry. Recall Ronald Dworkin asserted that abuse of discretion can be seen that certain crimes are acceptable if the judge's principles are skewed enough.

Instead a controversial legal concept known as 'Inherent Powers' is used. "Inherent power is that which the court necessarily possesses irrespective of constitutional provisions. Such power may not be abridged by the legislature. Inherent power is essential to the existence of the court and the orderly and efficient exercise of the administration of justice. Through its inherent power the court has authority to do all things that are reasonably necessary for the proper administration of justice." Beard v. N.C. State Bar, 320 N.C. 126, 129 (1987) "The court has the inherent authority to do what is reasonably necessary for the proper administration of justice." Beard at 130.

Judicial Branch is not held accountable to the Constitution nor enacted laws. Much like their use of 'Ex Mero Motu' acting by their mind's own accord. There is no justice, service or protection of citizens when the Judicial Branch has the self-appointed power to do as it pleases in the name of their own self-preservation not justice.

In the same 10th District Wake

County (N.C.) Superior Court Judge Paul C. Ridgeway on September 15, 2011 side steps a ruling of a lower court that Public Officials / Agencies are not "private entities" and immune from liability by claiming the action is outside his jurisdiction. However, the aforementioned law is specific about how public officials are responsible for themselves and who they supervise.

The real issue in both of these cases is not the legislative law, that is specifically clear, the real issue is that these cases were brought against government, specifically the judicial branch, by private citizens represented pro-se. While that is assumptive it is a trend that is easily followed by court records.

Regardless, in both instances the cases were shot down not by the legislative law but by an abuse of discretion using very interruptive case law as a trump over legislative law, the law of the people. So you see they make up the law as they go along and rather than explain their abuse of discretion they often obfuscate in a dead language, calling their personal choices by the latin phrase, Ex Mero Motu. Ex Mero Motu translates as 'by my own accord [mind]' or defined in Black's Law Dictionary as "Creating an order to a grant a right to a party they are not specifically entitled to" and ergo depriving a party of a right they are entitled to. Most judges do not follow law. They follow cronyism within their faction of elite citizenry, an oligarchy paid for by the wealthy in gifts, bribes, favors, and campaign contributions unattainable by common citizenry. Specifically, both of these judges need to be replaced. Their corruption is far too obvious. Unfortunately it is not limited to Wake County, North Carolina. This is a national problem at both the state and federal levels.

It is because we have let factions take over the judicial branch leading the public to believe an education in law was a prerequisite for wisdom. This has been shown to be false and consider that not even our highest office, The President of the United States of America, has an educational qualification.

The courts were designed to be governed by WISE men or women of the community not people who pay dues to the BAR association.

Back to John Adams, his "Thoughts

on Government" (1776) discriminates the various functions of government into three branches —executive, judiciary, and legislative— and that they must be separated in order to prevent tyranny. Adams' <u>Defence of the Constitutions of Government of the United States of America</u> (1787) presented his thinking that the greatest dangers to any polity, a form or process of civil government or constitution, came from an unbridled democracy. Our Republic, a few representing the majority, he described as an unrestrained aristocracy capable of becoming an oligarchy. The antidote to these dangers was a strong executive. He spoke of this powerful executive as the "father and protector" of the nation and its ordinary citizens, for this person was the sole official with the independence to act in a disinterested manner with inherent powers.

While we see the President and governors vetoing matters originating from their respective legislative branch, what we do not see is the President or governors vetoing their respective supreme court and neither does the legislative branch. The Judicial Branch has the final say and full authority over government. This is absolute power that already is tyranny hiding obfuscated.

James Madison In Federalist #2 described the necessity of government, "Nothing is more certain than the indispensable necessity of government, and it is equally undeniable, that whenever and however it is instituted, the people must cede to it some of their natural rights in order to vest it with requisite powers."

Three ideas from Madison state "But the most common and durable source of factions has been the various and unequal distribution of property. Those who hold and those who are without property have ever formed distinct interests in society." Further reading will lead to, "…the smaller the number of individuals composing the majority [opinion/authority], and the smaller the compass within which they are placed, the more easily they concert and execute their plans of oppression. Extend the sphere, and you take a greater variety of parties and interests; you make it less probable that a majority of the whole will have a common motive to invade the rights of other citizens[.]" In Federalist #14, "[elite citizenry] which have subverted the liberties of the old world, and as the proper antidote for the disease of faction, which have proved fatal to other popular governments, and of which alarming symptoms have betrayed by our own."

Abraham Lincoln is misquoted as writing and is most likely attributed to John Nicolay, Lincoln's private secretary, who wanted to express the economic climate of the US some twenty years after Lincoln's assassination. This idea penned in 1896, despite the author, is a foretelling of today's circumstance.

"I see in the near future a crisis approaching that unnerves me and causes me to tremble for the safety of my country. . . . corporations have been enthroned and an era of corruption in high places will follow, and the money power of the country will endeavor to prolong its reign by working upon the prejudices of the people until

all wealth is aggregated in a few hands and the Republic is destroyed."
—*U.S. President Abraham Lincoln, Nov. 21,* *1864*
(letter to Col. William F. Elkins)

Thomas Jefferson offered this advice, "The two enemies of the people are criminals and government, so let us tie the second down with the chains of the Constitution so the second will not become the legalized version of the first."

Translated, factions are dangerous and in a Republic like ours it is this voluntary lending of natural rights which is a necessary evil to be watched, scrutinized, made transparent and held accountable.

Recently the Supreme Court

complained because a camera was smuggled into their court room. In this age of technology we should have a channel dedicated to watching every court session. This new information age has the ability of democracy by the people because access is available to everyone. No court room should be anything less than transparent. And Judicial Immunity is an archaic concept created by Judges. There should be no immunity to deviate from the law.

The first consideration for reform is to break up the faction of elite citizenry that our forefather warned us about.

. . .

Therefore, under the Statesman Party the ideals that the Judicial Branch shall adhere to 'The Rule of Law." The rule of law will begin a strong foundation with four principles:

1. The laws are clear, stable, publicized and just. Evenly and equally applied to protect fundamental rights including the security of persons and property.
2. The process by which the laws are enacted, administered, communicated, and enforced are accessible, fair, and efficient.
3. Law is delivered justly by the adherence to legislation delivered timely by elected, competent, ethical, and independent representatives who are selected to be reflective of the makeup of the communities they serve.
4. The government and its officials, elected, appointed or hired, and its

agents as well as individuals and private entities are accountable to, by and under the law.

...

The Statesman party vows to work towards these resolutions.

1. Common Law, precedent cases, will be regulated to a five year limit such that it will either be legislated into law or it will expire as to relevance in future cases including cases subsequent that use it as its basis or precedent. Not becoming a law will not automatically usurp former decisions or exclusively allow for a new trial.
2. Judges will be limited to two terms to prevent entrenched corruption.
   a. An advancing judge, district to

superior, superior to Appellate/Supreme, state to federal will be limited by their final office.

b. Appointments made by the executive branch to a judgeship will be made from the existing pool of judges and in the case of district judges, that position will be filled by an elected official [current or previous] or former judge who, the appointed, waives his right to run in the next election cycle.

3. Judges will be elected from all citizenry based on popular opinions of wisdom and not limited to educational requirements of a faction or elite citizenry.

4. A trial by jury is a fundamental right and the show cause portion

of such demand for trial by jury requires a tribunal of a judge and two jurors for dismissal but not independently dismissed by a presiding official. This tribunal will be in the presence of plaintiff and defendant with brief oral arguments to be limited to five minutes each with no cross examinations. The plaintiff first and defendant in response.

5. Failure to sign a Subpoena, in a calendared hearing or trial, will require an explanation for why the subpoena is not relevant in the interest of justice in the case.

6. The use of 'Ex Mero Motu' will have a requirement of justification and waives a judges right to "Judicial Immunity" allowing for civil or criminal cases to be

available against the prevalent Abuse of Discretion.

7. Judicial Immunity will only apply in Jury Cases.

8. A court ruling will be required to become public record within 45 days. [This will prevent the courts from kidnapping children in child custody disputes which presently are heavily gender biased.]

9. Transparency will be mandated by law. Courts will be recorded digitally by both audio and video and stored for a minimum of ten years or length of sanctions/punishments/sentencing plus 5 years.

10. All new laws or revised laws will be written in American English. The use of Latin or any other language shall be prohibited to

ensure that the majority language of these United States are the clearest and most comprehendible to any citizen.

"Happiness is not a reward - it is a consequence. Suffering is not a punishment - it is a result."

- **Robert Green Ingersoll**

2 MENTAL HEALTH

Reform and solutions begin on page thirty-seven (37).

The Department of Health and Human Services, a part of the executive branch of government, is severely broken because of a lack of leadership and a culture of 'status quo' ignoring and violating laws. How can we know if our current system doesn't work if we aren't using it? What good is creating new laws in a culture were law is consistently ignored and accountability completely absent?

Around 1931, researchers suggested a "balloon theory" postulating that the mental institutions and the prisons are part of an interrelated system. Balloon theory claims, and history has proven, that when one part is pressed in as with a balloon that there will be a bulge elsewhere on the balloon wall. While naysayers dispute the validity of this theory, what was perceived as a truth was that by the 1980's the mental health system could no longer afford to keep institutions running. With some questionable practices in the 1970s by psychiatrists, politicians saw depopulating the institutions as quick money.

The abandoned facilities made cheap properties for beds for the correctional system. The mental health systems systemized dismantling occurred just in time to bolster the corrections system in the short term. Now, prisons are our new mental institutions while real criminals and offenders go free and unpunished.

Mental health services did not improve by calling the sufferers of mental illness criminals. Quite contrary, the prison populations are over populated with marginal offenders who because of their mental illnesses will not be released back into the general public. This is a travesty of civil liberties. We punish people for being sick and do not provide even the minimum of services. All the while the predators of civilized people, felons and criminals exploit, steal, and victimize law abiding citizens.

The stigma that surrounds mental illness is in part because of the labeling of these very real medical conditions. The terminology of a Mental Disorder needs to be legislated out. Bipolar Disorder is an illness accepted as a mental illness. It is not a disorder any more than cancer is a disorder or Alzheimer's is a disorder. A medical illness will be labeled as such Bipolar Illness or Borderline Personality Illness.

Services for our mentally ill

population already exist in law but are not enforced internally by our own government. We have here in North Carolina the State Consumer and Family Advisory Committee whose purview is to investigate and report on the service array in North Carolina. Since 2006, eight years have passed and no such investigation or report has occurred. $30,000 dollars a year is spent on a committee of twenty one people who are clueless on their responsibilities.

The Joint Oversight Committee over the Department of Health and Human Services is the working 'check and balance' between the legislative branch and the judicial branch. Their power being the control of money which funds programs. This committee meets regularly to listen to updates generated internally while ignoring the media and constituents that continually report a system that is utterly broken from top to bottom. Representative Hollo, a joint chair of this committee, stated that the legislative branch was powerless to hold the executive branch accountable. This apathetic attitude is the exact lack of leadership that destroys democracy and breaks down our 'checks and balances' in a three part government.

Since the Department of Health and Human Services [executive branch] does not enforce or follow law, then the legislative branch corrects this by suspending funding for services not being provided in accordance to laws.

The simple idea is that representatives of the people enacted laws to support the population. There is an expectancy that these laws will be followed and if it is found by the legislative branch that these laws are not being followed by the executive branch then money paid to these divisions and agents of services to the community are to be suspended until compliance with law is established or has the Attorney General file charges.

The initial argument will be that cutting services to a community is a human rights violation, however, the cause of this suspension of services is because the services being funded for are not being provided as the law outlined.

Simply put, if a gardener is paid for lawn care including grass, trimming and hedges. Then providing only grass cutting and trim is not the completion of the contract and services will not be paid until the hedges are done as well. While very simplified this is the power structure that exists to ensure conformity to law that is our government's promise to the people. Law without enforcement is nothing.

Apathy and stigma, including self-stigma, is a major hurdle in the public perception of mental illness. The landscape and media are advertising mental health issues in very little detail. The most effective way to educate our population about mental health concerns is through our education system.

Basic graduation requirements include math, science and broad topic humanities. Psychology, especially abnormal psychology and social psychology are not addressed in secondary education. Concepts like 'different not less' have broad reaching impacts over bullying, removing stigma, and supporting whole health concepts of body and mind.

Biology II, Chemisty II, Physics, Trigonometry and Calculus are excellent courses for future engineers and some researchers. But a greater percentage of high school students would be better served by alterative options in the humanities. Just like basic Algebra or Biology a requirement for Psychology with a component of mental health introduction should be a basic requirement. Education and information are the tools to break down the barriers of stigma, apathy and discrimination.

. . .

The Statesman party vows to initiate a new paradigm of education that teaches not just what to think but how to think.

Members of the Statesman Party will utilize the vested power of law utilizing funding discretion to guarantee to our citizenry that laws will be followed by our government.

Members of the Statesman Party will work towards legislation that creates high school students to become a more collegiate and well-rounded student and future socially aware citizen.

Members of the Statesman Party will work to fulfill the promise of community services and to create Mental Health courts to place individuals in appropriate facilities and not imprison illness nor leave these illnesses untreated.

Funding for the State Consumer Advocate found in Section Two of the 122C:10-20 Laws will activate the Advocacy portion of law and guarantee citizens a right to appeal and be heard.

CIT Officers are Crisis Intervention Team Trained law enforcement that are supposed to be able to identify and react to mental illness. Deescalating a situation and getting the suspected person with a disability to appropriately trained care givers. However, currently in North Carolina it takes a Master's Degree to work in occupations regarding Mental Illnesses and yet there is a push for these high school graduates with Basic Law Enforcement training to spend 40 hours and become mental health screeners. While this sounds good in theory, the reality is that officers are not qualified. Law enforcement are ignoring families, patient histories and deciding on the spot, untrained and unqualified who is mentally ill and who is not. They are not to diagnose, they are to deescalate and transport to qualified evaluators. In North Carolina alone in the last two years there has been three deaths against people with known mental illnesses. This very important difference in both training and responsibility is a priority for the Statesman Party.

"Punishment is now unfashionable... because it creates moral distinctions among men, which, to the democratic mind, are odious. We prefer a meaningless collective guilt to a meaningful individual responsibility."

- **Thomas Szasz**

3 CRIME & PUNISHMENT

Reforms and new solutions begin on page fifty (50).

Like the indulgences of the fifteenth century where a quaestores [Latin for professional "pardoner"] would sell eternal salvation and the repentance of sins both past and future - supposedly based off of earned merits or good works. Modern day plea bargains are utilized by attorneys and district attorneys who are more concerned with cronyism, politics and the elite citizenry than a justice system or victims. The selling of plea bargains have become just the cost of conducting criminal enterprise at the expense of victimized law abiding citizens.

The United States of America once prided itself on a penal system that rehabilitated criminals and returned them to society. When this failed to work, a crackdown on crime occurred in the 1980s and 1990s. "Tough on Crime" and "War on Drugs" were the battle cry that helped in filling prisons and jails across the nation.

Recall that in that same time frame Mental Institutions were being shut down. The disenfranchised sufferers of mental illness then became part of the criminal population when minor nuisance crimes of the mentally ill began to reach the courtrooms. Combine those numbers and you have even greater numbers of inmates as our prisons become the new psychiatric holding areas not hospitals. The largest mental institution in the country is actually the Twin Towers of a county jail in downtown Los Angeles. The facility houses 1,400 convicted mentally ill patients in one of its two towers.

This overcrowding spurred a cry for

prisoner rights. While our volunteer military lived in cramp quarters defending our constitution and laws, those who committed crimes against those laws were getting sympathy that they were confined in too close quarters and didn't have enough personal space as is considered humane.

A navy bunk room housed 60 sailors in 667 square feet aboard the USS Conserver ARS-39. That is 11.1 square feet per person. An inmate in a North Carolina jail is 6' x 8' in single celling and equates to 48 square feet. Double bunks 24 square feet. And should they be triple bunked then civil rights activist start complaining about only 16 Square feet per criminal. We comfort the people breaking the laws better than our soldiers defending the laws.

In January of 2014, North Carolina

closed five prisons claiming a reduction in sentencing and need. The reduction in sentencing is the Judicial Branch of government selling crime by means of plea bargains. No longer are we a nation that punishes and rehabilitates criminals. Instead the Judicial Branch makes local attorneys and county coffers wealthier by selling crime and 'commemorative' sentencing. Commemorative because it means little to nothing except on a piece of paper sold for a few dollars.

In her 2006 thesis paper at North Carolina State University, Kylie Lynn Perrotta states "Sentencing guidelines were introduced to regulate judicial discretion and to assure equality in sentencing decisions for similarly situated offenders. However, some scholars argue that limiting judicial discretion under sentencing guidelines results in a transfer of discretionary power to prosecuting attorneys; providing prosecutors greater power in charging decisions and thereby undermining equality in sentencing."

This practice threw open wide the door of abuse and corruption. Judges elected to have wisdom over courts and juries have been removed from the system such that crime had been removed from citizen juries and placed in the hands of individuals. Lack of punishment followed.

A recent example is John Russell Stoutt III, North Carolina Public Offender # 392404. A career criminal with seven prior convictions is newly convicted of felony possession of a firearm by a felon and given a plea bargain sentence of 24 months by Wake County Assistant District Attorney

Jonathon Holbrook under the supervision of District Attorney Colon Willoughby.

The reality was that the criminal paid $1200 and was assigned a probation officer that gave him early release after 11 months. The criminal saw no imprisonment, was not rehabilitated, was not punished, and based on the decision of a high school graduate served 46% of his plea bargain, which was a greater bargain indeed for the criminal. During those eleven months the probationer was cited for improper towing of a motor vehicle meaning he tried to steal it by not filing the paper work with the DMV. A crime similar to some of his other convictions like Obtaining Property under False Pretense and two other convictions for worthless checks.

While on probation evidence of sexual offenses and exploitation of the mentally ill by illegal drugs was reported to the probationer's office. No investigation was ever initiated.

Instead of staying in the jurisdiction of his probation as mandated, the felon enjoyed motorsports in neighboring states by using an alias, Russell J. Stoutt, to participate in the events. The career felon continued his criminal enterprise of pimping and selling drugs. An activity which he had already been convicted of twice before; once for marijuana and once for cocaine. Despite irrefutable evidence the probation officer Laya Trotman, district 10, never revoked his probation. Instead she recommended and he received early release.

But her "Willful Failure to Discharge Duties" is common place and not limited to Trotman. In thirty years, there was never any rehabilitation and even after an eighth conviction he still has never spent an overnight in jail. This portion of his criminal history does not even include the other 28 arrests nor countless reports of sexual offenses and communicating threats. The reason is because crime pays.

The State of North Carolina has a recidivism rate of 57% which means for every 100 prison releases 57 of them will be arrested again within 2 years. Clearly showing that no rehabilitation is occurring. Why should we think that any rehabilitation is occurring? In the afore mentioned example Stoutt was not required any type of rehabilitation services and he did not go to prison for the crimes committed.

. . .

REDEFINE PLEA BARGAINS

Mostly applicable to non-violent crimes. In violent crimes, no plea bargain is available except as an incentive to report others and then a maximum of 20% relief could be negotiated for length of a maximum term.

A plea bargain would be limited to once per ten years and twice per life time. A plea bargain could guarantee no more than half of a sentence maximum under the same class as the offense.

If a criminal commits a class F felony, with a maximum of 41 months then a plea bargain can guarantee no less than 20.5 months.

In the case of non-violent crimes the sentence will be carried out in the convict's own home under ankle monitor arrest and at their own expense. A probation officer does not release a criminal found guilty by a jury and sentenced.

Consider the present system. Only an educated lawyer can be a judge. But a person with a GED can undermine a judge's sentencing and allow for early release.

. . .

HOUSE ARRESTS

It has been estimated that 1 in 31 Americans is a probationer. Roaming the streets business as usual. Their crime had a cost of business that included the courts but ultimately profited. Therefor crime pays.

The North Carolina Department of Public Safety reports that an average inmate costs $27,572 a year to detain and assumingly rehabilitate. The cost of electronic monitoring costs $3,588 a year to restrict and gps track convicted criminals.

Considering a recent commission finding that 8,500 new beds will need to be found. Using house arrest will provide these beds at the majority expense of the criminal. Using these numbers, we can compute a 204 million dollar savings, with electronic arrest versus imprisonment. That 204 million dollars could be used to remove the mentally ill populations from prison to a proper institution to effect training, education and integration into society mitigating their mental illnesses. Which would further reduce the number of prison beds required making only violent offenders imprisoned.

In 2011, North Carolina House Majority Leader Paul Stam, was quoted by ABC as saying, "We're not going to coddle criminals. We're going to put them in prison for the appropriate amount of time," [But] "if a criminal is willing to not be violent, we don't need to punish them as much as someone who is violent." Paul Stam is willing to reduce some "nonviolent" drug offenses from felonies to misdemeanors. Personal use drug offenses are already misdemeanors, meaning that selling drugs or trafficking drugs is for the wholesale victimization of abusers and their families. Destroying the support groups and infrastructures on interpersonal relationships. Exploitation is violence against the mind and emotions and drug abuse is physical harming the physiology of the victim. Drugs are socially destructive, physically and mentally harmful to reduce the severity of any drug crime is coddling to criminals.

The fundamental problem with this statement is that he was not just referring to drug offenses but also worthless checks, fraud, perjury and array of other crimes. Crime is an offense against another's liberties and ownership of self. These are all violent crimes, they strip their victims of dignity, security, and create emotional hardships that they would not have endured had they not been victimized. The idea that violent crime requires physical harm is designed only to limit punishment not protect victims.

But, these criminals who are not

repeat criminals, nor do they use physical violence or intimidation; these criminals can be under house arrest.

There is absolutely no reason that a plea bargain should ever allow a criminal free reign within the public. The cost of the electronic monitoring should be part of the conviction. This would allow a non-violent criminal to live in their own home. Responsible for their own costs of living. The rehabilitation will be at their expense and is a condition of ending their home arrest.

There should be no plea bargains, except to guarantee a sentencing within the appropriate structure on the appropriate end. Thus a Class F felon will not be plea bargained to a Class G, but could be plea bargained to the minimum time of a class F and house arrest. House arrest would require that the probationer remain in his own home at his own expense. The annual cost of the electronic monitoring device would be the responsibility of the convicted. The length of a punishment would not be waived at any point.

Rehabilitation and work status would be required as a term of the punishment. Any convict that was not at the appropriate locations as programmed in the tracking schedule would be immediately in violation and taken to prison for review.

This process would eliminate the need for most of the prison space currently in use and would serve to remove criminals from the population by restricting them to their own homes with travel time to occupations that would actually make them pay for the costs of their monitoring.

Their rights as humans would not be any more limited than if they were incarcerated in a jail. In fact the dispersion of inmates into their own homes would reduce jail violence, reduce prison exposure which is currently used as a social venue to link with other organizations and criminals for future criminal enterprises.

The family of the criminal could remain with the criminal. Having a strong family support group of spouse and children would be far more beneficial than a thug collective in the prison yard.

With jails now selling phone time and commissary money for amenities this has become a business instead of the rehabilitation and punishment system it was intended to be.

In addition, probationers should be

made to wear uniforms much like school uniforms imposed on children. This is to alert the public that these individuals are criminals and for non-criminals to be wary. Some will argue that this is public humiliation and creates shame or anxiety. But this is not just punishment, a uniform designates punishment. If they had not wanted to be punished then they should have adhered to the law. Consequently, there is no style to uniforms and therefor costs can be kept low to facilitate the need for their earned income to go towards rehabilitation.

. . .

HABITUAL CRIMINALS

Habitual Felon, in North Carolina, now means that a person has to be convicted on a felony charge four times before the D.A. has the choice to decide if they are habitual. What non-sense is this? If they have been convicted four times of felonies then they are habitual. A District Attorney should not get to choose.

Every time you are convicted of a crime your next crime should automatically be elevated to one level higher not of the new crime but of your highest level crime.

If you commit a class I felony, NC's lowest one and then get convicted of a class II misdemeanor, then you need to be sentenced to a Class H felony. The punishment does fit the crime. You are already a convicted felon that failed to be rehabilitated therefore you need more time away from society and more rehabilitation.

Since they will be under house arrest they are not over burdening a burgeoning prison system. They are out of the way of society. They can have friends over, family can watch them but they will meet all the restrictive requirements of house arrests. Limited travel, rehabilitation, counseling and a more lengthy sentence.

Failure to follow these simple rules for non-violent crimes will result in a 30 day lock up followed by a second offense of six months, and finally they will do their term in isolation. If they had wanted community and socialization then they would have stayed on and followed house arrest. They chose their own fate. Three chances to prevent isolating them from society is ample leniency for civilized society.

. . .

STOLEN VALOR

More and more cases of impersonators pretending to be veterans of our armed forces. Regardless of the reason for the ruse, from discounts to prestige, impersonating a defender of our nation should be an actionable offense. The punishment should be nothing less than the yearly salary of the rank being portrayed by the offender and community service to improve the environment among disabled veterans.

. . .

WILLFUL FAILURE TO DISCHARGE DUTY

Any government employee, having been found to have been trained or the employee and their supervisor, manager or director if training was inadequate, who is found to be ignoring or in violation of the laws of North Carolina shall be punished by no less than one month salary and termination from employment.

. . .

FLOATING PRISONS

If they had wanted to live in our society then they should have followed our society's rules. To pave the way for a successful future we must began to think outside of the box. We cannot keep doing things the way they have always been done. American ingenuity and creativity were the keystones to the past. Let's revitalize this part of our character.

Recently there was an article discussing building floating platforms as animal and plant life habitation. These designs were based off existing oil rig platform structures.

In conjunction with the house arrest solution for offenders this isolation prison is the follow up step to low cost punishment and incarceration. A habitat for prisoners that refuse to comply with house arrest. A structure such as this would offer the opportunity for a green and vibrant exile. The food would be provided by the inmates themselves and their survival or not would be based on their own rehabilitation.

Exile has long been the historical humane punishment. And while this concept sounds very science fiction, so did cell phones, satellites, GPS, and thousands of other things less than a quarter century ago.

This concept has not been visualized completely but has enough promise for further inspection and creative design.

An example of this idea can be found on the internet at

http://www.takepart.com/article/20

14/12/09/these-floating-sea-trees-could-be-oasis-wildlife-needs-people-take-over-their?cmpid=tp-fb

I was very skeptical for adding this 'futuristic' possible solution because I believe that most citizens are resistant to change as much as they long for it. Like stated elsewhere in this book, a politician looks to the next election and a statesman looks to the next generation. Time and technology march forward. To survive we must embrace that simple idea.

From Meriam-Webster Dictionary:

fac·tion[1]
    'fakSH(ə)n/
    Noun

1. a small, organized, dissenting group within a larger one, especially in politics.
2. A state of conflict within an organization; dissension.

4 FACTIONS

The concept of factions has been addressed in many of these chapters so does not need an in depth conversation here. Understanding the dangers of factions is important enough that a few pages will illustrate what a faction is and how they are dangerous.

The Statesman Party defines a faction as:

3. A caucus, cabal, bloc, camp, section, branch, wing, arm, clique or group of people that utilize infighting, dissension, dissent, strife, conflict, bickering, controversy and friction to accomplish disharmony, disunity, and schism for their own personal agenda, power and economic advantage which is separate and apart from the well-being of the whole.

Capitalism is all about equality and the ability of individuals to rise above their station and accomplish and acquire wealth beyond their fore fathers. In this pursuit it is important to band together with like-minded people and to work together for like-minded ideas.

What has happened is that as these factions have developed they have left the economic realm and have sought power in governmental affairs. President James Madison wrote in his Federalist Papers #10 about the dangers of factions.

It will be the duty of the statesman party to identify and remove factions from within government.

Corporations are not citizens.

Insurance companies cannot be allowed to decide if an insured agencies can follow a law or not; and when they do they shall be held culpable to aiding and abetting in that crime.

An association of lawyers cannot legislate themselves as elite citizenry to occupy and rule over one branch of our government.

Democracy is about equality of all persons and the Statesman Party is dedicated to ensure democracy considers the individual rights above any faction.

"All animals are equal, but some animals are more equal than others."

— George Orwell, *Animal Farm [a dystopian novel]*

Dystopia is defined as a society characterized by a focus on negative societies such as mass poverty, public mistrust, police state, squalor, suffering, or oppression, that society has most often brought upon itself.

5 ELITE CITIZENRY

Reform, ideation and solutions begin on the page seventy-two (72).

The opening quote has been a plague on human societies since our beginnings. Banding together under strong personalities evolved into the 'divine right of kings' and as kingdoms expanded and grew then came 'oligarchies.' The idea of oligarchies does not just include the premise of 'he who has the gold makes the rules' it also includes governance over the many by a special few called an 'elite citizenry' e.g. a noble class, board of directors, private society, or class of citizens.

In a capitalistic society we promote these collectives to get grand endeavors accomplished. However, as a democracy the needs of the whole outweigh the wants of a few. This last century in America has shown us that unchecked elite citizenry undermines the foundations of our beliefs and constitution.

. . .

CORPORATE PERSONHOOD

One such 'Elite Citizenry' are 'corporations' and they are not 'human entities' or 'natural persons.'

In our legal system we recognize that corporations can and should be allowed to utilize our court systems in dispute over property and trade rights. But there is a limit to the 'human rights' of a corporation.

In the Fourteenth Amendment to the United States Constitution, the law is interpreted as "under the designation of 'person' there is no doubt that a private corporation is included" and that "such corporations are merely associations of individuals united for a special purpose and permitted to do business under a particular name and have a succession of members without dissolution."

Important to add is that part of this concept where the 1888 courts ruled was 'permitted to do business' as in commerce not government. Corporations cannot make rules or local practices contrary or negligent to the laws of our federal and state authorities.

Add to this the very important concept of responsibility and accountability. Corporations being a collective of citizens have the rights AND responsibility of American citizens. Multi-nationals do not have rights beyond our American established rights and laws.

Since a citizen(s), a natural person(s), a human(s) stands at the top whether alone or in a group of any organization then the rights and or punishment of a corporation should never be separate and apart from its controlling authority. While corporations should be burdened with the expense of compensation for crimes so shall the officers, leaders, directors, and board be held equally accountable.

. . .

EMINENT DOMAIN

Placing 'eminent domain' under elite citizenry might seem a little out of place. However in 2013 in North Carolina a push was made to justify condemning a property for the use by the public. A new Statesman House Bill would make a jury of twelve common citizens a requirement to allow government to seize a property by condemning it in the name of the public use.

Condemning a property should be a matter of safety and ownership of said property should remain with whoever owns it originally. Recall the pursuit of happiness was about ownership of land by individuals not the public. Developers, religious factions, and politicians should never have the power to force the sale of property under any guise, especially one so vague as public use.

If a jury of citizenry agrees with government that a property shall be found detrimental to everyone then and only then shall it be cleared but ownership shall not be deprived of the title bearer.

. . .

CONGRESSIONAL PRIVLEDGE

Government is a collection of citizens whose purpose is to 'form a more perfect union, establish justice and promote general tranquility, provide for a common defense, promote the general welfare, secure the blessings of liberty for ourselves and our posterity.' Government is accountable to the people.

The Statesman Party shall endeavor to ensure that elected officials are not provided benefits or favor at the cost of citizens outside of their personal and family security and the duties of their office.

That elected and appointed officials shall have the same medical insurance requirements and accessibility as our military.

That Senators and Representative shall have the same retirement packages as afforded to our military leaders based on time in service and rank achieved.

The Statesman agenda will include a bill that guarantees that no privilege shall be legislated to benefit the employees of any separate part of government alone.

. . .

REPRESENTATIVE LIMITS

The Statesman Party shall endeavor

to create a term bill that limits participation in politics in any given capacity to 8 years or three election cycles for said position.

For example, a house representative is elected for two year terms thus they can be eligible for election four times in this capacity. Whereas a Federal Senator serves a term of six years thereby allowing for two election cycles. Our president is already limited to two four year terms.

The premise is to limit the amount of corruption and 'elite citizenry' from forming within government. Politics should never be a career path. However great leaders should be allowed to continue public services in multiple capacities.

Given the vast number of electable positions it is possible for a life time to be spent within government. What is needed is to remove the entrenched ideology of the few and to allow a constant flow of governmental authority from among the people.

. . .

CONGRESSIONAL ACCOUNTABILITY

Any congress who creates a budget, outside of times of war, that is in excess of 105% of the State or Federal Revenue shall forfeit their right to run for re-election or election or to be appointed to any government office in the future.

This will hold government fiscally accountable and ensure longevity of our state.

This will not prevent an excessive budget to counter circumstances deemed necessary for the protection of the citizenry. However it will remove the elected population who was unable to foresee or correct any occurring deficiencies.

"A government generally acknowledged as being in control of a nation and deserving formal recognition, which is symbolized by the exchange of diplomats between that government and the governments of other countries." - The American Heritage® New Dictionary of Cultural Literacy, Third Edition

6 SOVEREIGNTY

What happens when the government no long follows rules of law but are instead a facade of what is designed? Then is no longer sovern. The use of Inherent Powers and Ex Mero Motu to create an environment of abuse of discretion. In the absence of functioning government we are truly in a state of lackadaisical anarchy. There is no 'Serve and Protect' when the very institution of law has become apathetic or corrupt. Extending a blind eye while bought and paid for. So many Americans are uncomfortable and craving change but we are so detached from one another we feel helpless or powerless in our individualism. Time to stand together and demand change and hold government accountable.

The first thing required is to abolish the status quo. Both the Republican Party and the Democratic Party have ruled over states and nation with narrow agendas serving a very small slice of Americans. Like Roman coliseums politicians toss out bread and games and divert the attention of American's through media ownership.

There is no solution to legislate common sense. The individual American must understand that involvement is required. Fewer people read newspapers and TV stations are splintered into small factions that are meant to disorient and confuse the masses.

Citizens must take an interest in public affairs. To not do so is to allow yourselves to be ruled by evil men. The good of the whole is quite often also good for the individual. American democracy requires that American citizens begin to talk, communicate and know what their government is doing. Anything less is to abandon your children to a country owned not shared, to a justice system preached not practiced, and to a future of servitude and not independent.

Government of the people, by the people and for the people must first include participation of the people.

Si nescio quid est lingua. Quo uero expectamus obedire legi aut cohabitare pacifice simul.

- **Daniel Orr**

[*Latin for* - "If you do not know what the language is . How can we expect to obey the law , or to live together peacefully."]

7 IMMIGRATION & NATIONAL LANGUAGE

In any relationship, good communication is essential.

Solutions, ideation and reform begin on page eighty-seven (87.)

In the late 1970s America had an extreme shortage of nurses. One Canadian nurse came to America with her two year old son on a work visa. She arrived legally and continued her obligations to the medical community and aided many American patients. Her son grew up sixteen years in American schools with American friends learning American politics and idealisms. When he turned eighteen he was deported as an illegal alien back to Canada where he was born but didn't even remember.

Meanwhile, pregnant women enter this country illegally and then have a baby on American soil and automatically get immunity for their crime so they can raise their child to be an American. This criminal immigrant is now not only immune to deportation, she and her husband can reside and receive benefits of our already strained social service system. This infant child who has no culture, no concept of society or patriotism, acts as an anchor to allow perhaps good people to enter by illegal measures. No matter how you look at it, it's a crime. As this book has previously shouted 'Crime pays in America' and again this has to end.

. . .

Our country already has immigration laws. If these laws are not followed then first offenders shall be deported as per the law. Repeat offenders shall be a capital crime. If they can not follow the law to enter legally then they cannot be expected to follow the law once they have arrived.

. . .

There shall be established a National Language for the business of government. All laws shall be written in Standard American English. All warning labels and safety instructions shall be written in Standard American English. Standard American English shall be taught in all educational circumstance, except for foreign language classes. Standard American English will be used for all driving tests, immigration tests, tax forms, Social Security forms and any other government agency form. Failure to learn and understand Standard American English will not be a legitimized excuse for any failure of service or law infraction. Every citizen has the right to use and speak in any language they desire however all government business will ne in Standard American English without exception.

"For an economy built to last we must invest in what will fuel us for generations to come. This is our history - from the Transcontinental Railroad to the Hoover Dam, to the dredging of our ports and building of our most historic bridges - our American ancestors prioritized growth and investment in our nation's infrastructure." – **Cory Booker, New Jersey Senator.**

8 INFRASTRUCTURE

THE FUNDAMENTAL FACILITIES SERVING A COUNTRY, CITY, OR AREA, AS TRANSPORTATION AND COMMUNICATION SYSTEMS, POWER PLANTS, AND ROADS.

Jump to page ninety-eight (98) for the solutions / projects section.

From the Federal Highway Administration website, "The Interstate System has been called the Greatest Public Works Project in History. From the day President Dwight D. Eisenhower signed the *Federal-Aid Highway Act of 1956*, the Interstate

System has been a part of our culture—as construction projects, as transportation in our daily lives, and as an integral part of the American way of life. Every citizen has been touched by it, if not directly as motorists, then indirectly because every item we buy has been on the Interstate System at some point. President Eisenhower considered it one of the most important achievements of his two terms in office, and historians agree."

Beginning in 1919 with a military experiment on the Lincoln Highway, the idea that commerce, military, and private citizen transport would be essential to the vitality of American life. World War Two further demonstrated the advantages of a multiple lane traffic system. In 1956, the Federal

Government commissioned this grand progressive concept which like all great ideas would be hindered by nay-sayers, technology limitations, budget constraints and multitudes of minor complaints (ugly, useless, frivolous). In the end our Interstate system has proven to be one of our greatest achievements. It created jobs in its construction and allowed our industrial revolution to become a commerce evolution. Another grand idea needs to be considered to continue this advancement of our American infrastructure.

There are 2,605,331 miles of paved road in the United States. Vehicle lanes vary in width from 9 to 15 feet. The U.S. Interstate Highway System uses a 12 foot standard. Simplistic math for a broad generalization would create an area of 62,527,944 square feet taking into account two way traffic. Much, much more if you consider emergency lanes, parking lots, off ramps, {4, 6, 8} multiple lane roads and trails.

Recent experimentation in Idaho, where solar collection would be minimum as opposed to southern states, the results indicate that a solar system including roads, trails, and parking lots would produce more than three times our current energy consumption. But let's assume that is very optimistic and realize that if it's just one third (33%) true it produces our current energy consumption.

What else would it do? The Industrial Revolution taught us that replaceable machine components was a more efficient way to build things. The Information Age has taught us the value of multi-tasking. So imagine if roads were little public services factories. For a visual consider a shipping container as a 3D representation. The top of this equipment being a rigid hard surfaced road for traffic. Under that a solar array collection surface with LED panels arranged to provide traffic information. Lane markings, Speed Limits, Construction, Accidents, Weather Alerts even animal ahead warnings.

Then under this panel is the factory. The walls would be lined with fiber optics for communication and internet traffic. There could be water collection systems for rain run offs. Fresh water distribution and waste collections. All built in an efficient tubular structure with ease of access for maintenance, testing, and most of all upgrades.

These component road pieces would fasten together and be inserted into the ground. As technology improves or wear over time happens then road crews wouldn't spend weeks or months clogging up transit. Off sight the replacement parts would be built and a crew would show up unfasten and lift out the old section and insert the improved section in a matter of hours. The hard surface becomes immediately available while internal connections could be completed in safety and without interruption of services.

This out of the box concept built into a box would potentially have rewards like 'no more potholes' saving money for vehicle repairs, flats, and driver safety. There would be a

significant decrease in greenhouse
admissions since solar energy is the
cleanest. The system would be a
beginning infrastructure for electric
vehicles. Our national security would
improve because there wouldn't be a
centralized power creation location that
could be targeted by enemies. The
demand on oil would be greatly reduced
meaning cheaper logistic costs for
delivering products. Self-warming
means roads would be snow and ice free
and that would improve driver safety.

This new system would be decades
in the building creating jobs and
opportunities. Most importantly the
segmented system would provide
centuries of rapid upgradability. Our
science fiction dreams would become
modern landscapes not unlike the cell

phone and internet of the early 21st century.

. . .

The Statesman party vows to work towards these improvements.

Not as a civil engineer but as a representative of the Statesman party, our efforts would push technology in this area to improve the lives, safety, security, environment and finances of our citizens. We should stop building roads like advanced Romans and begin building roads like our modern engineering allows.

. . .

Interchangeable Highways & Service Distribution

While the solar highways are considered inefficient by many scientists the fact remains that building the infrastructure for an interchangeable parts replacement system will encourage growth in this technological field and prepare us for the necessary changes to come. Whether a section of solar road powers just its own section or adds to the power grid is irrelevant because that replaceable section in twenty years can quickly and efficiently be replaced by an updated model. The additional services of fiber optics, rain water run-off, fresh water distribution, and power grids makes these mini-service factories a great leap forward in civil engineering.

. . .

Floating Nature Reserves

As stated on pages 27 & 28, a conceptual idea for floating platforms based off of current oil rig designs could act as conservatories for avian and aquatic species. Combine this with some hydroelectric turbines utilizing ocean currents and we can begin to rebuild nature's populations and work to keep balance between technology and nature.

"Many American pundits and foreign policy experts love to depict themselves as crusaders for human rights, but it almost always takes the form of condemning other governments, never their own." - **Glenn Greenwald**

9 FOREIGN POLICY

Policy and approach begins on page one hundred four (104.)

The United States Military is not a humanitarian force nor a police force.

Our military is a deadly force to protect the Constitution, the rights and freedoms of OUR citizens.

The war in Iraq is not ensuring American Security. If the people of Iraq, Afghanistan, Russia, Somalia, Libya, Yemen or any other country become an unquestionable real threat to American lives exterior to those countries borders then the threat will be dealt with in extreme measures including but not limited to complete decimation of the country's infrastructure but is necessity demands their population. Not because we want to but because they left us no other choice but to compromise our security, rights laws, and beliefs by inaction. Compromise about the sanctity of our own soil is never an option.

The recent Ebola outbreak, President Obama has sent troops into Africa on a humanitarian mission. This is very unacceptable. The CDC, Center for Disease Control, and the WHO, World Health Organization, are government entities who exist solely for this purpose. No soldier, sailor or airmen should be expected to police a civilian population in our country or another. Should a country not want the assistance of the CDC and WHO, it is not the military's purview to protect a humanitarian effort. Should said country prefer to die from epidemic or plague that is their right and prerogative.

In Rwanda there was genocide. In Somalia, there were warlords. In Uruguay, dictator. In Northern Ireland, domestic terrorists/revolutionaries. In each case, the events in these foreign lands did not threaten the safety or sanctity of The United States of America ergo our presence is not legal nor reasonable.

In the circumstance of Iraq invading Kuwait, Kuwait was an ally and we responded as allies do. In the circumstance of Ukraine, they were not our allies and we responded with sanctions not military as non-allies do.

. . .

Incorporation not intervention

A country that shares our own ideology of a democratic republic that requests our aid as an official government act, would also be required to recompense for the cost of our involvement including the annexation of their own country into a territory belonging to us. Not because we are mercenaries but because the blood and lives of Americans is priceless and not to be expended trivially. The cost for their sovereignty is not to be gained by the loss of our young men and women or all of our tax dollars.

. . .

Tariffs and Fair markets

Any goods or services out sourced or imported to be utilized within our borders shall comply with our own labor laws. The producing country will have equal minimal wages or the products will be taxed for the difference. A foreign states accesses to natural resources is the advantage of their geographical region and does not play a part in the appraisal of creation of goods and services. However, and most importantly safety measures and wages do.

Any country that employees children below the age of 16 will not be allowed to sell products within the our state's boundaries.

No country shall be allowed to export to our State products whose value exceeds more than 125% of products they import from our state. Our goods and services shall be necessary for the global economic stability.

. . .

Foreign Debt

A very complicated and web like mess of loans taken out by the United States Government for services and currency speculation / stabilization. The full scope of foreign debt is beyond the author's immediate knowledge.

The Statesman Party will conduct business as to create no new foreign debt and current foreign debt shall be addressed annually and the amount of foreign aid provided to other countries and regions will be counted against foreign debt. There will be no more free American Dollars or resources to places that claim America owes them money.

. . .

Domestic Debt

Again another mix of borrowing from organizations which can be called factions using these loans as political pressure to affect the policies and direction of American politics.

The Statesman Party will conduct business as to create no new domestic debt and current domestic debt shall be addressed annually to affect reductions in all areas beginning with outside influences contrary to American sovereignty.

"If you set out to be liked, you would be prepared to compromise on anything at any time, and you would achieve nothing." - **Margaret Thatcher**

10 TRADITIONAL ARGUMENTS

The author is not a politician. Daniel Orr is a troubleshooter, fixer and leader. The Statesman Party ideals were created from the necessity of today with the wisdom of past generations. The Statesman Party presented here is not the 1977 National Statesman Party, a renaming of the Prohibition Party, but an entirely new and much needed alternative to our existing two party system.

There will always be the constant lobbying for gun control, abortion, religion and other divisions of our society. But it will be important to many about the author's current views and equally important to point out that as a member of the Statesman Party individual views may differ since these topic are not part of the party platform.

Our society is still here after 236 years because our private citizens are allowed to own guns, so punish criminal acts not tools. Abortion already has been argued and regulated to how long a pregnancy is allowed with the option of abortion. Religion in our country was intended to be a safe haven of personal beliefs as long as they did not impede on the beliefs of others.

The Statesman party agenda on these three topics is that no change in the current law or doctrine will occur. Not because these topics lack importance but because so much energy has been expended to create no change that it is evident we as a society are not yet ready to conform to a singular ideal. We have compromised all we are willing on both sides.

Therefore, the Statesman party will table these concerns to address far more immediate and solvable concerns as it is our responsibility to leave this country and the world better than how our parents left it to us.

Everything begins with just one person who believes, shares and works to an end. If we work together then me and others like me can help all of us create a better society. There can be no apathy in civil affairs if democracy is to survive.

ABOUT THE AUTHOR

Daniel Orr, Dano, is the average citizen. Earning a slightly more than median salary for over twenty-five years. He is a veteran of our armed forces, serving six years in the Navy. Volunteered as the head of parent/teacher organization for four consecutive years. After becoming disabled by Meniere's Disease, a balance disorder, uses his time to advocate for the rights of the seriously mentally ill in his home state of North Carolina. He is a member of NAMI – The National Alliance on Mental Illness and NCCASA – North Carolina Coalition Against Sexual Assault.

This book was written to point out some of the systemic failures of our society and to offer solutions not just complain. Dano is considering a 2016 run for the Governor Office in North Carolina if he can find the required approximately 88 thousand signatures on a petition of support. See the Appendix if you would like to help.

The formation of a Statesman Party is also in the works for those independents who found their voice in these pages and to those disenfranchised Republicans and Democrats that realize their party has deviated from their own beliefs and serve the few instead of us all.

BECOMING GOVERNOR OF NORTH CAROLINA

FROM:
HTTP://WWW.NCSBE.GOV/NCSBE/PORTALS/0/FILES
P/FILINGFACTSGOVCOS2016.PDF

FACT SHEET

Running for North Carolina Governor, Lieutenant Governor, and Council of State 2016 Election

1) **Which offices are in the Council of State? (N.C. Const. Art. III §§ 7(1), 8)**

- Secretary of State
- State Auditor
- State Treasurer
- Superintendent of Public Instruction
- Attorney General
- Commissioner of Agriculture
- Commissioner of Labor
- Commissioner of Insurance

2) How does a person's name get on the ballot for the primary election?
(NCGS §§ 163-106, 163-107, 163-108)

- Candidates must file a notice of candidacy with the State Board of Elections office and pay a filing fee of 1% of the annual salary of the office sought. Notice of candidacy forms may be obtained from the State Board of Elections office prior to the date on which candidates may commence filing.

- A candidate must be a registered voter of the same political party in which he or she intends to file (a person changing party affiliation must do so 90 days prior to the date the candidate files).

- At the time of filing, all candidates must file a certificate signed by the Director or Chairperson of the County Board of Elections where they are registered to vote at their current residential address in that county. The certification states the party with which the person is affiliated, and that the person has not changed party affiliation in the past 90 days.

North Carolina State Board of Elections Running for North Carolina Governor, Lieutenant Governor, and Council of State: 2016 Page 2

- The notice of candidacy includes questions about any previous felony convictions of the candidate, and will require a further report on those convictions if there are any. Active felons who have not had their citizenship rights fully restored (full completion of any felony sentence, including probation, restitution, etc.) are not eligible to be registered to vote or to run for elected office.

- A candidate may not file for more than one office in the same election.

- Candidates who have properly filed their notice of candidacy and paid the filing fee will have their names certified by the chairman of the State Board of Elections to the Secretary of State three days after the expiration of the filing period.
- A filed primary candidate who remains unopposed after the close of the filing period will be certified as his or her party's nominee without the need for a primary.
- The winners of the party primaries (or certified nominees, if unopposed) will be listed on the General Election ballot as the nominee of their party for the office they filed for.

3) When is the filing period? (NCGS §163-106(c))

- Begins: Noon on the second Monday in February of the year of the election, Monday, February 8, 2016.
- Ends: Noon on the last business day in February of the year of the election, Monday, February 29, 2016.

4) What if a candidate wants to run as unaffiliated with a political party?
(NCGS §§ 163-122, 163-123)

- If a candidate wishes to run unaffiliated, he or she should review North Carolina General Statute § 163-122 and fact sheet on running as an unaffiliated candidate.

- If a candidate wishes to run as a write-in, they need to review North Carolina General Statute § 163-123 and the fact sheet on running as a write-in candidate.

5) When are the elections? (NCGS § 163-1)

- Primary: The Tuesday after the first Monday in May preceding the general election, Tuesday, May 3, 2016.
- Second primary (will only be held in certain situations, and if requested by a candidate): The date will depend on whether any elections for federal office require a second primary.

For more information, see North Carolina General Statute
§ 163-111.
☐ General election: The Tuesday after the first Monday in November,
Tuesday, November 8, 2016.

89,366 Signatures required.

Please distribute and collect five (5) sheets or 100 signatures. Then mail same to 103 Northwood Road, Henderson NC 27536. Only by working together can we reclaim government for the citizens.

Daniel Wayne Orr

118

Saving America

PETITION TO CREATE A NEW POLITICAL PARTY (GS § 163-96 (a)(2))

WE, THE UNDERSIGNED QUALIFIED REGISTERED VOTERS IN _____ COUNTY HEREBY PETITION FOR THE FORMATION OF A NEW POLITICAL PARTY TO BE NAMED

Statesman Party AND WHOSE STATE CHAIRMAN IS Daniel Orr , RESIDING AT 103 Northwood Road AND WHO CAN BE REACHED BY

TELEPHONE AT 252-431-4387 Henderson, NC

27536

PURSUANT TO CHAPTER 163 OF THE GENERAL STATUTE PROVIDING FRAUDULENT OR FALSE INFORMATION, OR SIGNING THE NAME OF ANOTHER PERSON TO THIS PETITION IS A CLASS I FELONY.

BOE ONLY	Line No.	Print your name (Must be printed legibly)	Residential street address	ZIP code	Birth date (DD/MM/YYYY)	Signature
	1					
	2					
	3					
	4					
	5					
	6					
	7					
	8					
	9					
	10					
	11					
	12					
	13					
	14					
	15					
	16					
	17					
	18					
	19					
	20					

SUBMIT COMPLETED FORMS TO THE OFFICE OF (COUNTY) BOARD OF ELECTIONS.

Board of Elections use only

Page _____ of _____ pages   Batch No. _____   Date received ___/___/___

Daniel Wayne Orr

STATE BOARD OF ELECTIONS
6400 Mail Service Center • Raleigh, North Carolina 27699-6400

PETITION REQUEST FORM

Petition Name _____ (50 characters max)
Filing Date _____
Expiration Date _____
Required Signature Total _____

Petition Properties, check one:
- [ ] ABC
- [ ] Charter
- [ ] Municipal
- [ ] Filing Fee
- [ ] Bonds
- [ ] Repeal of Levy Tax
- [ ] School Tax
- [ ] Unaffiliated Candidate _____ (office running for)
- [ ] Write In Candidate _____ (office running for)
- [ ] New Political Party _____ (name of Party)

Subtype: Check one
- [ ] Municipal
- [ ] County
- [ ] District, 2 or more Counties
- [ ] Single County or Legislative District
- [ ] State

Organization _____ optional
Contact Name _____
Primary Phone _____
Secondary Phone _____ optional
Fax _____ optional
Email _____ optional
Contact Address _____
_____
_____

Requested By: _____ Date_____

Petition -001 8/13/2011

120

www.ingramcontent.com/pod-product-compliance
Lightning Source LLC
Chambersburg PA
CBHW050355280326
41933CB00010BA/1474